MW00896690

HVAC for Beginners [5 in 1]

The Comprehensive Guide to Ventilation, Heating and Air Conditioning Systems. Learn Installation, Maintenance, and Repair Techniques.

William Jocelyn

Copyright © 2023 by William Jocelyn

All rights reserved. No part of this publication may be reproduced, distributed, or transmitted in any form or by any means, including photocopying, recording, or other electronic or mechanical methods, without the prior written permission of the publisher, except in the case of brief quotations embodied in critical reviews and certain other noncommercial uses permitted by copyright law. In no way is it legal to reproduce, duplicate, or transmit any part of this document in either electronic means or in printed format. Recording of this publication is strictly prohibited, and any storage of this document is not allowed unless with written permission from the publisher. All rights reserved. The information provided herein is stated to be truthful and consistent, in that any liability, in terms of inattention or otherwise, by any usage or abuse of any policies, processes, or directions contained within is the solitary and utter responsibility of the recipient reader. Under no circumstances will any legal responsibility or blame be held against the publisher for any reparation, damages, or monetary loss due to the information herein, either directly or indirectly. The information herein is offered for informational purposes solely and is universal as so. The presentation of the information is without contract or any type of guarantee assurance.

The trademarks that are used are without any consent, and the publication of the trademark is without permission or backing by the trademark owner.

All trademarks and brands within this book are for clarifying purposes only and are owned by the owners themselves, not affiliated with this document.

TABLE OF CONTENTS

Book 1: Introduction to HVAC

Understanding the basics of heating, ventilation, and air conditioning

HVAC is a crucial technology for maintaining comfortable and healthful interior environments in residential, commercial, and industrial contexts. HVAC systems regulate temperature, humidity, and air quality, and they can have a significant impact on energy consumption, operating costs, and environmental sustainability.

This chapter will provide a comprehensive overview of the fundamentals of HVAC, including its components, principles, and applications. In addition, we will discuss the significance of energy efficiency and sustainability in HVAC technology, as well as the most recent developments and emerging trends in the industry.

Components of Heating, Ventilation, and Air Conditioning Systems

A HVAC system consists of four fundamental components:

The heating system is responsible for producing heat to soften the air within a structure. Furnaces, boilers, and heat exchangers are typical heating system varieties. The ventilation system is responsible for bringing in fresh air and removing stagnant air from a building. Air ducts, filtration, and blowers may comprise ventilation systems.

The air conditioning system in a structure is responsible for chilling the air within it. Air conditioning systems include central air conditioning, ductless mini-split systems, and window air conditioners. The control system is responsible for moderating the indoor temperature, relative humidity, and air quality. This may include thermostats, sensors, and other monitoring and adjusting devices for the HVAC system.

Fundamentals of HVAC

HVAC technology is founded on the thermodynamic principles that govern the transfer of thermal energy between objects and their surroundings. The three most important thermodynamic principles applicable to HVAC systems are:

Heat transfer is the transmission of thermal energy from one object or substance to another. Conduction, convection, and radiation are the three primary forms of heat transfer. Thermal capacity is the quantity of thermal energy that an object or substance can retain. Different materials have varying heat capacities, which can influence their ability to absorb or discharge thermal energy.

Controlling the temperature of a space or object by adding or subtracting thermal energy. This can be accomplished through a variety of means, including heating, cooling, and ventilation.

Implementations of HVAC

HVAC technology has numerous applications in a variety of contexts, including:

In residences and apartments, HVAC systems are utilised to regulate the temperature, humidity, and air quality. Residential HVAC systems typically consist of central air conditioning, heat furnaces, and ductless mini-split systems.

In order to maintain comfortable and healthy indoor environments in office structures, retail spaces, and other commercial settings, HVAC systems are utilised. In addition to zone control, air filtration, and humidity control, these systems are typically more complex and sophisticated than residential systems.

HVAC systems are utilised in a variety of industrial environments, including manufacturing facilities, data centres, and hospitals. These systems are frequently designed to meet specific temperature, humidity, and air quality requirements, and they may include air filtration, humidity control, and energy recovery.

HVAC Energy Efficiency and Environmental Sustainability

HVAC systems can have a significant impact on energy consumption, operational costs, and environmental sustainability, making energy efficiency and sustainability crucial considerations. Among the most important factors influencing the energy efficacy and sustainability of HVAC systems are:

System design is essential for optimising the energy efficacy and sustainability of HVAC systems. This could involve building orientation, insulation, and airtightness.

Equipment selection can also have a significant impact on energy efficiency and sustainability when it comes to HVAC systems. This may involve selecting heating and cooling equipment that is energy-efficient, as well as ventilation systems that utilise heat recovery and other innovative technologies.

Regular HVAC system maintenance and service can help assure optimal performance and energy efficiency. This may involve cleansing air filters, inspecting ductwork for leakage, and verifying refrigerant levels.

Recent Developments and Evolving Technologies

The HVAC industry is ever-changing, with new technologies and innovations emerging frequently. Among the most recent trends and emerging HVAC technologies are:

Smart thermostats: Smart thermostats learn user preferences and adjust temperature and humidity settings accordingly, resulting in increased comfort and energy efficiency.

Variable refrigerant flow (VRF) systems: Variable refrigerant flow (VRF) systems use advanced refrigerant technology to provide individualised temperature control in various areas of a building, resulting in enhanced energy efficiency and comfort.

Energy recovery ventilation (ERV) systems: Energy recovery ventilation (ERV) systems use heat exchangers to transfer heat and humidity between incoming and outgoing air, resulting in enhanced energy efficiency and interior air quality.

Solar-powered HVAC systems: Solar-powered HVAC systems utilise solar panels to generate electricity that can be used to power HVAC equipment and reduce reliance on the infrastructure, resulting in reduced operating costs and enhanced sustainability.

Types of HVAC systems and their components

Heating, ventilation, and air conditioning are abbreviated as HVAC. There are a variety of HVAC systems that accomplish these objectives. The primary kinds are:

Forced-air central systems are the most prevalent HVAC system. They use a furnace or heat pump to generate heated or cooled air, which is then distributed throughout the residence via a system of ducts and ventilation. The essential elements are:

- Utilises fuels or gas to heat air.
- Refrigerant is used to produce frigid air in an air conditioner.
- Air handler: A device that forces air through ducting.

- A system of metal or plastic pipelines that distributes conditioned air to every chamber.

- Registers and grilles are vents that supply each room with heated or chilled air.

- Split systems include an outdoor condenser unit and an indoor air handler unit connected by refrigerant lines. They are capable of both chilling and heating. Components consist of:

Compressor and outdoor coil are contained in the condenser. Refrigerant is condensed during the refrigeration cycle. The indoor coil evaporates and expands refrigerant for cooling purposes. Also absorbs air's heat during the heating cycle. The air handler includes both a ventilation fan and a filter. Air is circulated over the interior coil.

Heat pumps: Similar to split systems, but more efficient because they can provide both heating and cooling by operating in reverse. Components consist of:

- Outdoor compressor device
- Internal air handling device
- Four-way reversing valve: permits refrigerant to travel in either the heating or cooling direction.

- Additional heating: Typically, electric resistance heat is used to supplement heating on extremely frigid days.

Boilers: Heat water circulated through radiators or baseboard heaters with steam or hot water. Components consist of:

- Produces heated water or vapour for thermal purposes. Typically petrol or oil-fueled.
- Radiators distribute heat throughout a space.
- Pipes: Transports heated water or vapour throughout the system.
- Pump that circulates heated water through the piping.

Radiant heating: heating elements or ducting embedded in floors or walls that radiate heat. Beneficial for hard-to-heat regions. Components consist of:

- Electric resistors, hot water or steam tubes, or refrigerant-based ducting embedded in the floor, ceiling, or walls serve as heating elements.
- Thermostats and zone controls.

Individual room devices that provide both heating and ventilation are known as unitary systems. Components consist of:

- The condensing unit is composed of a refrigerant compressor and an outdoor coil.
- This coil absorbs and releases heat to provide cooling or heating.
- Air is circulated over the evaporator condenser by the fan.
- A louvred enclosure houses and directs airflow to components.

Each of these HVAC systems has advantages and disadvantages in terms of efficiency, comfort, installation cost, maintenance requirements, and application. When selecting and specifying the most suitable HVAC system, HVAC designers and contractors consider factors such as home size, configuration, climate, and requirements.

Thermostats, filters, duct insulation, duct sealing, air handlers, air exchangers, humidifiers, dehumidifiers, and zoning systems are also essential HVAC components. Proper maintenance, routine replacement of filters and other components, and periodic professional service can help ensure that an HVAC system operates safely and efficiently for a long time.

Energy efficiency and sustainability considerations

The HVAC industry is one of the world's largest energy consumers, accounting for roughly 40 percent of energy consumption in commercial and residential structures. The design, installation, and operation of HVAC systems must therefore incorporate energy efficiency and sustainability considerations. In this chapter, we will examine the essential energy efficiency and sustainability factors for optimising HVAC systems, such as system design, equipment selection, maintenance, and emerging technologies.

Planning Considerations

For HVAC systems to maximise energy efficiency and sustainability, proper system design is essential. Among the most important design considerations are:

- Building orientation can maximise passive solar heating and cooling, thereby reducing the need for energy-intensive HVAC systems.

- Insulation: Adequate insulation can reduce heat loss and gain, thereby reducing HVAC system workload and enhancing energy efficiency.

- Proper airtightness reduces air leakage and infiltration, thereby enhancing energy efficiency and indoor air quality.

- Ventilation: Through strategies such as natural ventilation, demand-controlled ventilation, and heat recovery ventilation, proper ventilation design can enhance interior air quality while minimising energy use.

Equipment Selection Considerations

Selecting the proper HVAC equipment is crucial for optimising energy efficiency and sustainability. Among the most important equipment selection factors are:

- High-efficiency heating and cooling equipment, such as heat pumps and variable refrigerant flow (VRF) systems, can drastically reduce energy consumption and greenhouse gas emissions.

- Advanced ventilation equipment, such as energy recovery ventilation (ERV) and demand-controlled ventilation (DCV) systems, can simultaneously enhance interior air quality and reduce energy consumption.
- Advanced controls and sensors, such as programmable thermostats and occupancy sensors, can optimise the performance and energy efficiency of HVAC systems.

Maintenance Considerations

Regular HVAC system maintenance and service is essential for optimal performance and energy efficiency. Among the most important maintenance considerations are:

- Regular replacement of air filters can improve indoor air quality and HVAC system energy efficiency by reducing HVAC system labour.
- Management of refrigerants: Proper management of refrigerants, including routine detection and repair of leaks, can increase energy efficiency and reduce greenhouse gas emissions.
- Regular ductwork inspection for leakage and damage can improve energy efficiency and indoor air quality.

Emerging Technologies

The HVAC industry is ever-changing, with new technologies and innovations emerging frequently. Among the most recent trends and emerging HVAC technologies are:

- Smart thermostats: Smart thermostats learn user preferences and adjust temperature and humidity settings accordingly, resulting in increased comfort and energy efficiency.

- VRF systems: VRF systems use advanced refrigerant technology to provide individualised temperature control in various areas of a building, thereby enhancing energy efficiency and comfort.

- ERV systems: ERV systems utilise heat exchangers to convey heat and humidity between incoming and outgoing air, thereby enhancing energy efficiency and indoor air quality.

- Solar-powered HVAC systems: Solar-powered HVAC systems utilise solar panels to generate electricity, which can be used to power HVAC equipment and reduce reliance on the infrastructure, resulting in reduced operating costs and enhanced sustainability.

Safety guidelines and best practices for HVAC work

Installation, repair, and maintenance of heating, ventilation, and air conditioning systems are just a few of the many tasks associated with HVAC labour. While these duties are necessary for ensuring optimal internal environments, they pose significant safety risks to HVAC technicians and others in the area. In this chapter, we will discuss some of the most important safety guidelines and best practises that HVAC technicians should adhere to in order to reduce the likelihood of accidents and injuries.

General Safety Guidelines

A number of general safety guidelines should be followed by HVAC technicians to ensure safe and effective HVAC work:

- Personal protective equipment (PPE): When working with HVAC equipment, proper PPE, including gloves, safety eyewear, and respiratory protection, must be worn at all times.

- Tools must be used in accordance with the manufacturer's instructions, and technicians must be trained in proper tool use and safety procedures.
- Heavy equipment and materials should be lifted and transported using proper lifting techniques, such as hoisting harnesses or dollies.
- Electrical safety: HVAC technicians must be trained in electrical safety procedures and must always switch off equipment's electricity before performing maintenance or repairs.

Installation Safety Instructions

The installation of HVAC systems can pose significant hazards to the safety of technicians and others in the area. Among the most important installation safety guidelines are:

- Wiring and grounding must be installed according to manufacturer specifications and local electrical codes.
- Ventilation should be implemented correctly to prevent carbon monoxide and other dangerous gases from accumulating in a building.

- To prevent environmental damage and health hazards, refrigerants must be handled and disposed of according to EPA regulations.
- HVAC equipment should be located in areas that are both secure and easily accessible for maintenance and repair.

Guidelines for Maintenance and Repair Safety

HVAC system maintenance and repair can also pose significant safety hazards to technicians and others in the area. Among the most important maintenance and repair safety guidelines are:

- Lockout/tagout procedures should be followed to prevent accidental equipment activation during maintenance or repair work.
- To prevent environmental damage and health hazards, refrigerant should be handled and disposed of according to EPA regulations.

- Ladders should be used in accordance with the manufacturer's instructions and installed on stable surfaces to prevent falls.
- During maintenance and repair work, adequate ventilation should be provided to prevent exposure to hazardous gases and particulates.

Guidelines for HVAC Work

In addition to following safety guidelines, HVAC technicians can follow several best practises to ensure safe and effective HVAC work:

Effective communication between HVAC technicians, building administrators, and other stakeholders can assist in the identification of potential safety hazards and the prevention of accidents. Regular training and education can assist HVAC technicians in keeping abreast of the most recent safety guidelines and best practises.

Regular quality control tests can aid in identifying potential safety hazards and ensuring that HVAC systems are operating effectively and safely. Continuous improvement: To ensure the utmost level of safety on the job, HVAC technicians should continuously review and enhance their safety procedures and practises.

Book 2: HVAC Installation and Maintenance

Planning and preparing for HVAC installation

For HVAC installations to be successful and meet the requirements of the building's occupants, careful planning and preparation are essential. In this chapter, we will examine some of the most important factors to consider when planning and preparing for HVAC installations, such as assessing building requirements, selecting equipment, identifying installation challenges, and ensuring compliance with local building codes and regulations.

Analysing Building Demands

Assessing the building's requirements is the first stage in planning and preparing for HVAC installation. Among the most important considerations are:

Size and configuration of the building have an effect on the required size and type of HVAC system. The number of building occupants, as well as their activities and schedules, will affect the building's heating, cooling, and ventilation requirements.

The insulation, windows, and doors that comprise the building envelope will affect the heating and cooling loads of the structure. The intended use of the building, such as commercial, residential, or industrial, will influence the HVAC system specifications.

Choosing Equipment

After assessing the building's requirements, the next step is to choose the appropriate HVAC equipment. Among the most important considerations when selecting equipment are: High-efficiency HVAC equipment can significantly reduce energy consumption and operating costs over the system's lifetime. Size and capacity of the equipment: To guarantee optimal performance and efficiency, the size and capacity of the equipment must match the requirements of the building.

Type of Equipment: The type of equipment, such as a central air system, heat pump, or ductless mini-split, will depend on the requirements of the building and the owner's preferences. Advanced equipment features, such as programmable thermostats, variable-speed fans, and air purifiers, can improve the system's comfort and energy efficiency.

Recognising Installation Obstacles

To ensure a successful HVAC installation, each installation presents its own unique challenges that must be identified and overcome. Among the most important installation challenges to consider are:

Access to the building: Access to the building, including parking and cargo areas, must be considered so that equipment can be delivered and installed in a safe and efficient manner.

Existing infrastructure: The existing electrical and ductwork infrastructure must be evaluated to determine if modifications or enhancements are necessary to accommodate the new equipment. The building's configuration, including the placement of equipment and ductwork, must be meticulously planned to ensure optimal performance and efficiency.

Local building codes and regulations must be carefully reviewed and adhered to in order to ensure compliance and avoid hefty fines or penalties. Ensure that local building codes and regulations are followed.

It is essential to comply with local building codes and regulations to ensure that HVAC installations are safe, energy-efficient, and meet the requirements of building occupants. Among the most important codes and regulations to contemplate are:

Electrical codes must be observed to ensure that wiring and grounding are installed safely and correctly.

- Mechanical codes: Mechanical codes must be observed to ensure the safe and proper installation of HVAC equipment and ductwork.
- Energy codes: Energy codes must be followed to ensure that HVAC systems are energy-efficient and meet local standards for energy efficiency.
- Environmental codes must be followed to ensure that refrigerants and other HVAC equipment are safely handled and disposed of.

Step-by-step guide to installing HVAC systems

Installation of heating, ventilation, and air conditioning (HVAC) systems requires meticulous planning, precise execution, and attention to detail. This chapter will provide a step-by-step guide for installing HVAC systems, including site preparation, equipment installation, and system testing and balancing.

Step 1: Site Preparation

Installation of an HVAC system begins with site preparation. This entails:

- The work area must be cleansed of any debris, equipment, or other materials that could impede the installation.
- Protecting the building: Floors and walls should be covered with protective materials to prevent damage to the building during the installation procedure.
- In order to facilitate future maintenance and repairs, access panels should be implemented in the ducting and other HVAC components.

- Testing the electrical system: The electrical system should be tested to ensure that it can power the new HVAC system safely and adequately.

Installation of Equipment

After the site has been prepared, the HVAC equipment must be installed. This entails:

- The air exchanger or furnace should be connected to the ductwork and installed in a central location, such as the cellar or attic.
- The condensing unit or heat pump should be connected to the air handler or furnace and installed outside the building.
- The ductwork should be installed according to the manufacturer's instructions and the local building codes and regulations.
- Registers and grilles should be implemented in every room to facilitate ventilation and temperature regulation.

Step 3: System Testing and Balancing

After the equipment has been installed, the system must be tested and calibrated to guarantee optimal performance and efficiency. This entails:

- Using the proper testing equipment, the ductwork and refrigerant lines should be inspected for leakage.
- Airflow testing: The airflow through the ductwork should be measured and adjusted as required for optimal performance and efficiency.
- Temperature testing: The temperature of the air circulating through the system must be measured and adjusted as necessary to ensure maximum comfort and efficiency.
- The building's humidity levels should be measured and adjusted as necessary to ensure optimal comfort and efficiency.

Best Installation Procedures for HVAC Systems

In addition to the steps enumerated above, HVAC technicians can follow the following best practises to ensure successful and effective HVAC installations:

Effective communication with building proprietors can help identify any special requirements or preferences that should be taken into account during the installation process. To ensure optimal performance and efficiency, HVAC equipment must be installed per the manufacturer's instructions.

To ensure safety and avoid costly fines or penalties, HVAC installations must adhere to local building codes and regulations. Ongoing maintenance and repair: Ongoing maintenance and repair can extend the life of the HVAC system and assure its optimal performance and efficiency.

Maintaining your HVAC system to maximize efficiency and longevity

Regular maintenance is required to ensure the efficacy and longevity of HVAC systems. In this chapter, we will examine some of the most important HVAC maintenance duties that building owners and HVAC technicians can perform to maximise the efficacy and longevity of HVAC systems.

Air Filter Maintenance

HVAC systems rely heavily on air filters for efficacy and efficiency. Filters that are dirty can restrict ventilation, diminish performance, and increase energy consumption. Among the essential air filter maintenance duties are:

Filters should be replaced routinely, typically every one to three months, depending on the type of filter and the frequency of use. The proper filter should be selected based on the requirements of the building and the HVAC system.

Reusable filters should be cleansed regularly in accordance with the manufacturer's instructions. Filters should be inspected for any breaches or openings that could allow unfiltered air into the system.

Coil Maintenance

Coils are another essential HVAC system component that requires routine maintenance. A decrease in efficacy, an increase in energy consumption, and premature equipment failure can result from dirty coils. Among the essential coil maintenance duties are:

Regular coil cleaning: Typically, coils should be cleansed every six to twelve months to remove grime and detritus that can accumulate on the surface. The appropriate cleansing method must be selected based on the type of coil and the amount of grime and detritus.

Coils should be inspected for leakage or damage that could reduce efficacy or cause equipment failure. Coating the coils: Coating the coils with a protective coating can prevent the accumulation of grime and detritus on their surface.

Routine Ductwork Maintenance

The ductwork is another essential HVAC system component that requires routine maintenance. A duct system that is dirty or damaged can reduce efficiency, increase energy consumption, and degrade indoor air quality. Among the most important ductwork maintenance tasks:

Regular ductwork cleaning: Typically, ductwork should be cleansed every 3 to 5 years to remove dust, detritus, and other contaminants that can accumulate inside. Sealing leaks and gaps: Leaks and gaps in the ventilation should be sealed in order to prevent air leakage that can decrease efficiency and interior air quality.

Insulating ductwork can prevent heat loss or gain, which can decrease efficiency and increase energy consumption. The ventilation through the ductwork should be measured and adjusted as necessary to ensure optimum performance and efficiency.

Best Maintenance Practises for HVAC Systems

In addition to performing routine maintenance, HVAC technicians and building proprietors can maximise the efficacy and longevity of HVAC systems by adhering to the following best practises:

Regular system inspections: Routine system inspections can aid in identifying potential problems before they become severe. Using high-quality components: Using high-quality components can help ensure optimal system performance and longevity.

Keeping comprehensive documents of maintenance and restorations can aid in tracking the system's performance and efficacy over time. Upgrades to the system on a regular basis:

Upgrading the system with advanced features and technologies can boost performance, efficiency, and indoor air quality.

Troubleshooting common issues and performing repairs

HVAC systems are complex and susceptible to a variety of problems throughout their lifetime. In this chapter, we will discuss some of the most common HVAC system problems, as well as how to troubleshoot and remedy them.

Common HVAC Issues

Among the most frequent problems that HVAC systems can encounter are:

- Inadequate airflow: Inadequate airflow can be caused by unclean air filtration, improperly designed ducting, or faulty fans or blowers.
- Inconsistent temperatures: Inconsistent temperatures can be caused by improper thermostat settings, air leakage in the ductwork, or faulty dampers or registers.
- High energy costs may be the result of inefficient equipment, conduit leakage, or inadequate insulation in the building envelope.

- Strange sounds: Strange sounds may be caused by missing or damaged components, deteriorated bearings, or faulty fans or blowers.

Resolving HVAC Problems

When HVAC problems arise, troubleshooting can help determine the underlying cause of the issue and the best course of action. Among the essential troubleshooting procedures are:

The first step in troubleshooting is to identify the problem's symptoms, such as odd disturbances, inconsistent temperatures, or high energy expenses. Examining the air filter: Examining the air filter is frequently the first step in diagnosing HVAC problems, as unclean filters can cause a variety of issues.

Inspecting the apparatus, such as the air handler, furnace, and condensing unit, can help identify any visible damage or evidence of deterioration. Checking the thermostat can help identify any incorrect settings or malfunctions that may be causing the issue.

Repairing HVAC Systems

Once the problem's primary cause has been identified, it may be necessary to perform repairs to resolve the issue. Typical HVAC repairs include:

Replacing air filters: Replacing air filters is one of the most common and straightforward HVAC repairs that can be performed. Cleaning coils, such as the evaporator coil or condenser coil, can enhance performance and efficiency.

- Sealing air leakage: Sealing air leaks in the ductwork can help to increase efficiency and decrease energy usage.
- Component repairs or replacements: Component repairs or replacements, such as fans, blowers, or compressors, may be required for more severe problems.

Best Methods for HVAC Troubleshooting and Maintenance

In addition to the procedures enumerated above, HVAC technicians and building proprietors can follow the following best practises to ensure successful troubleshooting and repair of HVAC issues:

Regular maintenance: Regular maintenance can aid in preventing issues from arising in the first place and identifying potential problems before they escalate into significant problems. To ensure the optimal performance and longevity of the equipment, repairs and maintenance should be performed in accordance with the manufacturer's instructions.

For more complex or severe problems, it may be necessary to engage a professional HVAC technician to perform the necessary repairs. Keeping records: Keeping detailed records of repairs and maintenance can help monitor the system's performance and efficiency over time, as well as identify recurring problems that may require additional attention.

Book 3: Ventilation Technology

Principles of indoor air quality and ventilation

Indoor air quality (IAQ) is a crucial aspect of building design and operation, as it has a substantial impact on occupant health, comfort, and productivity. In this chapter, we will examine the fundamentals of IAQ and ventilation, including the factors that influence IAQ, the significance of ventilation, and strategies for enhancing IAQ.

Factors influencing IAQ

Indoor air quality can be affected by a variety of variables, such as:

- Indoor environments can accumulate pollutants such as dust, pollen, and substances, which have a negative impact on IAQ.
- High humidity can contribute to the development of mould and fungi, while low humidity can cause parched skin and respiratory issues.

- Ventilation: Inadequate ventilation can contribute to the accumulation of indoor pollutants and moisture.
- Temperature: Extreme temperatures can negatively affect the comfort and health of building occupants, while inadequate temperature control can promote the development of mould and pathogens.

Vitality of Ventilation

Ventilation is essential for maintaining excellent IAQ because it helps remove contaminants and moisture from indoor environments. Some important advantages of ventilation include:

- Removing pollutants: Ventilation can assist in removing pollutants such as dust, pollen, and substances from indoor environments, thereby enhancing IAQ and decreasing the risk of health issues.
- Ventilation can aid in reducing the moisture levels in indoor environments, thereby preventing the development of mould and fungus.
- Improving occupant comfort and productivity, proper ventilation can help to maintain comfortable temperature

and humidity levels in indoor environments, thereby enhancing occupant comfort and productivity.

- Energy efficiency: Adequate ventilation contributes to energy efficiency by reducing the demand for heating and cooling.

Methods for Enhancing IAQ

There are a number of strategies HVAC technicians and building proprietors can implement to enhance IAQ, including:

- Source control involves identifying and eliminating or reducing the sources of pollutants in indoor environments, such as by using non-toxic cleaning products and reducing the use of chemicals.
- Increasing ventilation rates can assist in removing pollutants and moisture from interior environments, thereby enhancing IAQ and occupant comfort.
- Technologies for cleansing the air, such as air filtration and air purifiers, can assist in removing pollutants from indoor environments.

In addition to preventing mould and mildew growth and enhancing occupant comfort, humidity control can help prevent the growth of mould and mildew in indoor environments.

Best Practises for Indoor Air Quality and Ventilation

In addition to the strategies enumerated above, HVAC technicians and building proprietors can follow the following best practises to ensure optimal IAQ and ventilation:

- Regular maintenance: Regular maintenance of HVAC equipment can assist in identifying and resolving potential IAQ and ventilation issues prior to their escalation into significant problems.
- Compliance with local regulations and building codes can help to ensure that ventilation rates meet minimum requirements for the health and safety of occupants.
- Regular surveillance of IAQ can aid in identifying prospective problems and tracking the efficacy of IAQ and ventilation strategies.
- Education and communication: Educating building occupants about indoor air quality (IAQ) and ventilation can help to promote good IAQ practises and encourage cooperation in maintaining good IAQ.

Types of ventilation systems and their components

There are a variety of ventilation systems that can be used to enhance indoor air quality and maintain healthy, comfortable environments. This chapter will examine the various varieties of ventilation systems and their components, as well as their advantages and disadvantages.

Systeme de ventilation naturelle

Natural ventilation systems rely on the natural movement of air to ventilate interior spaces. These systems rely on passive design features to facilitate ventilation and require no mechanical equipment. Common natural ventilation system components include:

Openable windows and doors can be used to promote natural ventilation by allowing fresh air to enter and stagnant air to exit the building. Building orientation and design can be optimised to promote natural ventilation, such as by positioning windows and doors to take advantage of prevailing breezes.

Atria and courtyards can promote natural ventilation by establishing a central space that allows air to circulate throughout the building. Natural ventilation systems are advantageous due to their low cost, energy efficacy, and simplicity. However, external factors such as climatic conditions and the neighbouring environment can limit their effectiveness.

Systems of Mechanical Ventilation

Mechanical ventilation systems provide ventilation for indoor environments using mechanical equipment. There are two primary categories of ventilation systems: exhaust ventilation and supply ventilation.

Exhaust ventilation systems: Exhaust ventilation systems remove stagnant air from interior spaces and replace it with outside air. Common exhaust ventilation system components include fans, ducting, and vents.

Supply ventilation systems: Supply ventilation systems introduce outdoor air through dedicated supply ducts or the HVAC system into indoor environments. Fans, air filters, and ducting are prevalent components of supply ventilation systems.

In addition to their ability to provide consistent and controlled ventilation, mechanical ventilation systems are also effective at removing pollutants and moisture from indoor environments. Nevertheless, their energy consumption and expense can be greater than natural ventilation systems.

Hybrid Ventilation Systems

Hybrid ventilation systems provide ventilation for indoor environments by combining natural and mechanical ventilation systems. These systems can be designed to maximise the advantages of both natural and mechanical ventilation systems while minimising their disadvantages. Common hybrid ventilation system components include:

Controls and sensors: Using sensors and controls, indoor air quality can be monitored and ventilation rates adjusted accordingly. Dampers can be used to regulate the airflow between natural and mechanical ventilation systems. Fans and ductwork can be utilised to supplement natural ventilation with mechanical ventilation when necessary.

Flexibility, energy efficiency, and the ability to provide consistent ventilation while taking advantage of natural ventilation opportunities are all advantages of hybrid ventilation systems. Nevertheless, their complexity and cost may exceed those of natural or mechanical ventilation systems alone.

Best practises for the design and installation of ventilation systems

In addition to selecting the appropriate form of ventilation system, HVAC technicians and building proprietors can observe the following best practises to ensure optimal ventilation system design and installation: Ventilation systems should be sized appropriately so that they provide adequate ventilation without utilising excessive energy.

Air filtration: Ventilation systems should incorporate air filters to eradicate indoor pollutants and contaminants. Regular maintenance should be performed on ventilation systems to ensure optimal performance and efficiency.

Ventilation systems should comply with local regulations and building codes to safeguard the health and safety of occupants.

Ventilation load calculations and system design

Maintaining excellent indoor air quality and occupant health and comfort necessitates a properly designed ventilation system. Ventilation load calculations, which are used to determine the quantity of ventilation required to maintain optimal internal air quality, are an essential aspect of ventilation system design. In this chapter, we will examine the principles of ventilation load calculations and system design, including the factors that influence ventilation loads, the methodologies used for ventilation load calculations, and the ventilation system design considerations.

Aspects that Influence Ventilation Load

Ventilation load refers to the quantity of outdoor air needed to maintain optimal domestic air quality. Numerous variables can influence ventilation rates, including: The number of occupants in a building can impact ventilation burdens, as more occupants require more ventilation on average.

The type and intensity of activity in a building can impact ventilation burdens, as more strenuous activities generate more pollutants and moisture.The building envelope, including the type and quality of insulation, can influence ventilation loads by influencing the amount of heat transfer between the interior and outdoor environments.

Conditions atmosphériques: Conditions atmosphériques can effect ventilation loads by influencing the quantity of outdoor air required for ventilation.

Methods for Calculating Ventilation Load

Depending on the complexity of the building and the intended level of precision, a number of methods are available for calculating ventilation loads. Common techniques include:

The simplified ventilation rate method is a straightforward and simple method for calculating ventilation loads based on the number of building occupants and the sort of building activity.

The indoor air quality procedure is a more complex method for calculating ventilation loads that takes into account a variety of factors, including pollutant sources, outdoor air quality, and occupant sensitivity.

Modelling in detail: Modelling in detail involves the use of computer simulations to model the interior environment and calculate ventilation loads based on a vast array of input parameters.

Considerations in Ventilation System Design

Once the ventilation load has been calculated, the system design must be considered to ensure that the ventilation system is sized and configured appropriately to meet the ventilation load requirements. Important ventilation system design considerations include:

Location of external air intakes external air intakes should be located in locations free of pollutants and other contamination sources.

Type of ventilation system: The type of ventilation system, such as natural or mechanical ventilation, must be chosen based on the ventilation burden requirements and the building's specific requirements.

The selection of ventilation equipment, such as fans and air filters, should be based on the ventilation load requirements and the level of energy efficiency sought.

The ventilation ductwork's design should be optimised for minimal pressure losses and effective air distribution.

Ventilation Load Calculation and System Design Best Practises

In addition to the aforementioned principles, HVAC technicians and building proprietors can observe the following best practises to ensure accurate ventilation load calculations and system design:

The optimal performance and efficacy of ventilation systems can be ensured through routine maintenance. Ventilation systems should comply with local regulations and building codes to safeguard the health and safety of occupants.

Education and communication: Educating building occupants about ventilation and IAQ can help to promote and encourage good IAQ practises and cooperation in maintaining good IAQ. Regular surveillance and control of ventilation system performance can aid in identifying potential problems and optimising system efficiency.

Air distribution systems and their components

Air distribution systems are a crucial component of HVAC systems, as they are responsible for distributing conditioned air throughout a structure and ensuring the highest level of interior air quality and comfort. This chapter will examine the various forms of air distribution systems, their components, and their advantages and disadvantages.

Air Distribution System Types

Depending on the requirements of the building and the intended level of control over interior air quality and comfort, various varieties of air distribution systems can be used in HVAC systems. These are some prevalent categories of air distribution systems:

All-air systems are the most prevalent form of air distribution system and are typically found in commercial and industrial structures. These systems rely on a central unit to condition and distribute air throughout the building via ductwork and air diffusers.

Air-water systems are hybrid air distribution systems that integrate air distribution with a water-based heating or conditioning system. Typically, these systems are installed in larger structures with complex HVAC requirements.

Radiant systems: Radiant systems use a network of pipelines or panels to distribute heating or cooling to various zones within a structure. These systems are typically utilised in residential or small commercial structures, and they can provide greater energy efficiency and convenience than all-air systems.

Systems of Air Distribution Components

Air distribution systems consist of a number of essential components, each of which plays a crucial role in preserving optimal interior air quality and comfort. Typical air distribution system components include:

Air handlers are responsible for conditioning and distributing air throughout an entire structure. Typical components consist of a fan, filtration, and heating or chilling elements.

Ductwork is used to convey conditioned air from the air receiver to various zones throughout the building. A variety of materials, including sheet metal, fibreglass, and flexible materials, can be used to construct ductwork.

Air diffusers are utilised to distribute conditioned air from the ductwork into the interior space. There are various kinds of air diffusers, such as ceiling diffusers, floor diffusers, and wall-mounted diffusers. Dampers: Dampers are used to regulate airflow through ductwork, allowing for greater control over interior air quality and comfort.

Advantages and Restrictions of Air Distribution Systems

Air distribution systems provide numerous advantages, including:

- By providing consistent ventilation and air filtration, air distribution systems contribute to the maintenance of optimal indoor air quality.
- Air distribution systems can help to maintain consistent temperature and humidity levels throughout a building, enhancing the wellbeing of the occupants.
- Air distribution systems can be designed to be energy-efficient, thereby reducing operating expenses and environmental impact.

Nevertheless, air distribution systems have some limitations, such as:

- Complexity: Air distribution systems can be difficult to design and implement, necessitating great care for optimal performance.
- Maintenance: Air distribution systems require regular maintenance to ensure optimal performance and efficiency.
- Designing and installing air distribution systems can be expensive, especially in larger buildings with complex HVAC requirements.

Best practises for the design and installation of air distribution systems

In addition to selecting the right type of air distribution system and adhering to best practises for system design and installation, HVAC technicians and building proprietors can follow the following best practises to ensure optimal air distribution system performance:

Sizing: Air distribution systems should be sized appropriately to ensure that they provide adequate ventilation and air distribution without excessive energy consumption. To remove contaminants and allergens from indoor environments, air distribution systems should include air filters.

Regular maintenance should be performed on air distribution systems to ensure optimal performance and efficiency. Air distribution systems should comply with local regulations and building codes to safeguard the health and safety of occupants.

Installation, maintenance, and repair of ventilation systems

Installation, maintenance, and repair of ventilation systems must be performed correctly to ensure optimal interior air quality and occupant convenience. In this chapter, we will examine the fundamentals of ventilation system installation, maintenance, and repair, including installation considerations, the significance of regular maintenance, and common ventilation system repair issues.

Considerations for Ventilation System Installation

It is essential to implement ventilation systems correctly to ensure optimal performance and efficacy. Important ventilation system installation considerations include:

- System design: The ventilation system's design should be optimised to satisfy the building's specific requirements and the intended level of interior air quality.
- The selection of ventilation equipment, such as fans and air filters, should be based on the ventilation load requirements and the level of energy efficiency sought.
- Ventilation ductwork should be designed to minimise pressure losses and maximise air distribution efficiency.
- Ventilation systems should comply with local regulations and building codes to safeguard the health and safety of occupants.

Routine Upkeep of Ventilation Systems

Regular ventilation system maintenance is essential for assuring optimal performance, energy efficiency, and the health and wellbeing of occupants. Important ventilation system maintenance duties include:

- Air filters should be replaced consistently in order to maintain optimal air quality and energy efficiency.

- Periodically cleaning ductwork to remove grime, pollen, and other contaminants that can accumulate over time.

- Fans and actuators should be routinely inspected to guarantee their optimal performance and efficiency.

- Calibration of sensors and controls: Periodic calibration of sensors and controls is necessary to assure accurate measurement and control of indoor air quality and ventilation rates.

Common Ventilation System Maintenance Issues

Despite routine maintenance, ventilation systems may experience problems requiring repair. Common ventilation system repair problems include:

- Due to wear and strain or inadvertent damage, ductwork can become damaged, resulting in air leakage and decreased system efficiency.

- Fan or motor failure: Fans and motors can fail as a result of mechanical fatigue or electrical issues, resulting in a decrease in system performance and efficiency.

- Sensor or control issues: Due to electrical issues or component failure, sensors and controls can malfunction, resulting in inaccurate measurement or control of interior air quality and ventilation rates.

Best Practises for Installation, Maintenance, and Repair of Ventilation Systems

In addition to adhering to the aforementioned principles, HVAC technicians and building owners can follow the following best practises to ensure successful ventilation system installation, maintenance, and repair:

The optimal performance and efficacy of ventilation systems can be ensured through routine maintenance. Ventilation systems should comply with local regulations and building codes to safeguard the health and safety of occupants.

Education and communication: Educating building occupants about ventilation and IAQ can help to promote and encourage good IAQ practises and cooperation in maintaining good IAQ.

Regular surveillance and control of ventilation system performance can aid in identifying potential problems and optimising system efficiency.

Troubleshooting common ventilation issues

Indoor air quality (IAQ) and occupant health and comfort depend heavily on ventilation systems. Ventilation systems, like any other mechanical system, may encounter problems requiring troubleshooting and repair. This chapter will examine common ventilation issues and their respective troubleshooting techniques.

Inadequate Airflow

A prevalent ventilation problem is inadequate circulation. Inadequate ventilation can result in poor interior air quality, unfavourable temperatures, and increased energy consumption. Some frequent causes of inadequate ventilation include:

- Dirty air filters can reduce the quantity of fresh air entering a building by restricting the circulation.

- Clogged ductwork: Clogged ductwork can diminish airflow, resulting in inadequate ventilation and indoor air quality.
- Damaged fans or motors: Damaged fans or motors can reduce the airflow through the system, resulting in inadequate ventilation.

Technicians should check air filters, inspect ductwork for obstructions, and inspect fans and motors for damage to diagnose issues with inadequate ventilation. Regular maintenance, such as replacing air filters and cleansing ducts, can help prevent ventilation issues.

Excessive Noise

Another common ventilation issue is excessive commotion, which can be caused by several factors, including:

- Loose or damaged ductwork: Loose or damaged ductwork can result in air leaking out of the system, resulting in commotion.
- Unbalanced ventilation: Unbalanced ventilation can result in excess pressure, which can cause commotion.
- Damaged fans or motors: Damaged fans or motors can result in an increase in operational commotion.

Technicians should inspect ductwork for damage or leakage, balance the ventilation system, and inspect fans and motors for damage in order to troubleshoot excessive noise issues.

Poor IAQ

Poor IAQ can be caused by a variety of ventilation issues, such as:

- Inadequate ventilation: Inadequate ventilation can result in poor IAQ because the building does not receive enough fresh air.
- Dirty air filters: Dirty air filters can enable contaminants to circulate throughout the building, thereby diminishing the indoor air quality (IAQ).
- Damaged ventilation equipment: Damaged ventilation equipment can reduce the ventilation system's efficacy, resulting to poor indoor air quality (IAQ).
- Technicians should inspect the ventilation system for damage or malfunctions, replace soiled air filters, and modify ventilation rates as necessary to resolve IAQ problems.

Extremely High Energy Consumption

High energy consumption is another prevalent ventilation issue that can be caused by a variety of factors, like:

Inadequate system design can result in excessive energy consumption because the system is not optimised for energy efficiency. Damaged or inefficient equipment: Damaged or inefficient equipment can contribute to high energy expenses by consuming excessive energy. Dirty air filters and congested ductwork are examples of poor maintenance that can reduce system efficiency and increase energy consumption.

Technicians should inspect the system for damaged or inefficient components, optimise system design for energy efficiency, and perform routine maintenance tasks, such as air filter replacement and duct cleansing, to troubleshoot high energy consumption issues.

Advanced ventilation technologies and emerging trends

As the significance of indoor air quality (IAQ) and occupant health and comfort increases, so do the development of innovative ventilation technologies and the emergence of new trends. This chapter will examine the most recent ventilation technologies and trends, such as energy recovery ventilation, demand-controlled ventilation, and intelligent ventilation systems.

Recovery of Energy Ventilation

Energy recovery ventilation (ERV) is an innovative ventilation technology that recovers and transmits energy from exhausted air to incoming air. ERV systems utilise a heat exchanger to transfer heat and moisture from the outbound air to the incoming air, thereby reducing the amount of energy necessary to heat or chill the incoming air. ERV systems can enhance indoor air quality, reduce energy consumption, and reduce operating expenses.

Demand-Controlled Mechanical Ventilation

DCV is a ventilation technology that modifies ventilation rates based on a building's actual occupancy and pollutant levels. DCV systems measure CO_2, humidity, temperature, and other pollutants with sensors and adjust ventilation rates accordingly. DCV systems can enhance indoor air quality, reduce energy consumption, and reduce operating expenses.

Intelligent Ventilation Systems

Combining advanced ventilation technologies with internet-connected sensors and controls, intelligent ventilation systems are a growing trend. Optimising IAQ and energy efficiency, intelligent ventilation systems can adjust ventilation rates based on occupancy, outdoor weather conditions, and other factors. Smart ventilation systems can also provide real-time surveillance and control of the ventilation system, enabling building proprietors and HVAC technicians to swiftly and effectively identify and resolve issues.

Air Filters of Superior Performance

Emerging air filters can improve indoor air quality by capturing smaller particles and pollutants than conventional air filters. Specialised filters, such as HEPA filters, are utilised by high-efficiency air purifiers to capture particulate as small as 0.3 microns, including allergens, pathogens, and viruses. Air filters with a high efficiency can enhance IAQ and reduce the risk of airborne diseases.

Ultraviolet Germicidal Irradiation

UVGI is an emerging technology that employs ultraviolet light to disinfect the air and surfaces in a building. UVGI systems utilise UV-C light to eliminate bacteria, viruses, and other microorganisms, thereby reducing the danger of airborne diseases. UVGI systems can be installed as part of the HVAC system or as standalone devices, and they can be combined with other ventilation technologies to enhance IAQ.

Book 4: Heating Technology

Principles of heating systems and energy sources

Heating systems are an integral part of any HVAC (Heating, Ventilation, and Air Conditioning) system, as they provide warmth and comfort to building occupants. In this chapter, we will examine the fundamentals of heating systems and the various heating energy sources, including fossil fuels, electricity, and renewable energy.

Fundamentals of Heating Systems

Based on the transfer of thermal energy from a heat source to a heat absorber, heating systems function. Typically, the heat source is a furnace, boiler, or heat pump that converts fuel or electrical energy into thermal energy. Typically, the heat sink in a structure is the air or water, which absorbs the thermal energy from the heat source and distributes it throughout the structure.

A heating system's efficacy is determined by its capacity to transfer thermal energy from the heat source to the heat sink.

The efficacy of a heating system can be affected by the type of heat source, the distribution system, and the building envelope insulation.

Types of Heating Energy Sources

There are a variety of energy sources used to heat buildings, such as fossil fuels, electricity, and renewable energy sources.

Fossil Fuels

For heating buildings, fossil fuels such as natural gas, oil, and propane are a common source of energy. Typically, fossil fuel heating systems utilise a furnace or boiler to convert the fuel's chemical energy into thermal energy. While fossil fuels are a reliable and cost-effective energy source, they also have environmental impacts, such as air pollution and greenhouse gas emissions.

Electricity

Electricity is a common source of energy for heating structures, particularly in regions where fossil fuels are scarce. Typically, electric heating systems use resistance heating, which converts electrical energy to thermal energy. Although electric heating systems are pure and efficient, they can be more expensive to operate than heating systems that utilise fossil fuels.

Renewable Sources of Energy

The use of renewable energy sources, such as solar, geothermal, and biomass, is becoming increasingly popular in heating systems. Typically, heat exchangers or other technologies are used in renewable energy heating systems to extract thermal energy from the environment or from biomass fuel sources. Renewable energy heating systems can be a cost-effective and environmentally favourable alternative to fossil fuel heating systems.

Heating System Distribution Networks

A heating system's distribution system is responsible for distributing thermal energy throughout the structure. The most prevalent varieties of heating distribution systems are forced-air systems, hydronic systems, and radiant heating systems.

Air Pressure Systems

Forced air systems utilise a furnace to heat air, which is then distributed throughout the building via a network of ducts and ventilation. Common and cost-effective heating systems, forced air systems can be less efficient than other distribution systems.

Hydronic Systems

Hydronic systems utilise a furnace to heat water, which is then distributed throughout the building via a network of pipelines and radiators. Hydronic systems are efficient and can provide distributed heating, but their installation costs may be higher than those of forced air systems.

Radiant Heating Techniques

To heat a building, radiant heating systems employ a network of pipelines or electric heating elements installed in the floor, walls or ceiling. Radiant heating systems are effective and can provide zonal heating, but their installation can be more expensive than compressed air or hydronic systems.

Types of heating systems and their components

Heating systems are a vital component of any HVAC (Heating, Ventilation, and Air Conditioning) system, as they provide warmth and comfort to building occupants. This chapter examines the various forms of heating systems and their components, such as furnaces, boilers, heat pumps, and radiant heating systems.

Furnaces

Furnaces are a common form of heating system that utilise a fuel source to produce heat, such as natural gas, oil, or propane. There are two types of furnaces: forced air and gravity-based. In order to distribute heat throughout a building, forced air systems use a compressor to convey warm air through a network of ducts and ventilation, whereas gravity-based systems rely on the natural convection of warm air.

A furnace is comprised of a heat exchanger, a burner, and a compressor. The function of the heat exchanger is to transfer heat from the fuel source to the air. The burner ignites the fuel, while the compressor distributes the heated air throughout the structure.

Boilers

Boilers are another common form of heating system that use a combustible source to produce heat, such as natural gas, oil, or propane. Boilers heat water, which is then distributed via a system of pipelines, radiators, or radiant heating.

A boiler consists of a heat exchanger, a burner, a circulator pump, and a control system. The function of the heat exchanger is to transfer heat from the fuel source to the water. The burner ignites the fuel, whereas the circulator pump transports heated water throughout the distribution system. The control system regulates the boiler's temperature and operation.

Warmth Pumps

Heat pumps are a form of heating system that can also provide ventilation. Heat pumps use electricity to transport heat from one location to another, as opposed to directly producing heat. Both air-source and ground-source heat exchangers are possible.

A heat pump is comprised of an indoor unit, an outdoor unit, and a refrigerant. The evaporator coil within the interior device absorbs heat from the indoor air. The compressor and condenser coil, which release heat into the outdoor air, are housed in the exterior unit. Heat is transferred between the interior and outdoor devices by the refrigerant.

Radiant Heating Techniques

Radiant heating systems are a form of heating system that heats a building using a network of pipelines or electric heating elements installed in the floor, walls or ceiling. Radiant heating systems may be electric or hydronic.

Hydronic radiant heating systems utilise a furnace to heat water, which is then circulated through a system of pipelines, radiators, or radiant floors. A hydronic radiant heating system is comprised of a boiler, circulator pump, control system, and distribution system.

Electric radiant heating systems heat a building with electric heating elements installed in the floor, walls or ceiling. A radiant electric heating system consists of heating elements, a control system, and a distribution system.

Heating load calculations and system design

Heating load calculations are essential to the design of an energy-efficient, cost-effective, and comfortable heating system for building occupants. In this chapter, we will examine the principles of heating load calculations and the heating system design components, including equipment dimensions, duct design, and zoning.

Calculations of Heat Load

Heating load calculations are used to determine the quantity of heat required to maintain a building's interior at a comfortable temperature. The size and configuration of the building, the insulation of the building envelope, the type and number of windows and doors, and the local climate are all considered in heating load calculations.

There are a number of methods for calculating heating loads, including the Manual J method, which is widely employed in the HVAC industry. The Manual J method calculates the heat loss and heat gain in a building, which is used to determine the size and capacity of the heating system.

Aspects of System Design

After calculating the heating load, the next stage is to design a heating system capable of meeting the heating load requirements. A heating system's design consists of equipment dimensions, conduit design, and zoning.

Equipment Sizing

The measurement of equipment is a crucial aspect of heating system design. Oversized equipment can result in inefficient operation, while inadequately sized equipment can result in insufficient thermal performance. The heating burden calculation determines the size and capacity of the heating equipment, such as a furnace, boiler, or heat pump.

Duct Design

The design of ducts is another essential element of a heating system. The design of the duct system can affect the efficiency and efficacy of the heating system. Ducts are used to distribute heated air throughout a structure, and the design of the duct system can affect the heating system's efficiency and effectiveness. The design of the ducts should account for the size and configuration of the building, the thermal load requirements, and the capacity of the equipment.

Zoning

Zoning is an optional but advantageous feature of heating system design. Different areas of a building can be heated independently through the use of zoning, which can increase energy efficiency and occupant comfort. Through the use of multiple thermostats and dampers in the ventilation system, it is possible to create zones.

Installation and Maintenance of System

Installation and maintenance are essential for the efficacy and longevity of a heating system. Installation must be performed by a licenced and experienced HVAC technician in accordance with local building codes and manufacturer guidelines. Regular maintenance, such as air filter replacement and system cleansing, can contribute to the optimal performance and durability of a heating system.

Distribution systems and their components

HVAC (Heating, Ventilation, and Air Conditioning) systems rely on distribution systems to provide conditioned air to building occupants. This chapter will examine the various distribution system types and their components, such as ductwork, air handlers, and registers.

Ductwork

A network of pipelines or conduits that distributes conditioned air throughout a building is called ductwork. A variety of materials, including sheet metal, fibreglass, and flexible plastic, can be used to construct ductwork. The size and structure of the ductwork are determined by the size and layout of the building and the HVAC system's design.

Ductwork is comprised of ducts, elbows, transitions, and dampers. Ducts are the primary air distribution channels within a building. Transitions and elbows are used to alter the direction of the ducts or to connect different sections of ductwork. Dampers are used to control the airflow through ducts.

Air Handlers

Air handlers are HVAC system components that condition and distribute conditioned air throughout a building. Air handlers may be standalone units or integrated into a larger HVAC system. Air handlers may include filters, coils, compressors, and controls, among other components.

Filters are utilised to remove airborne contaminants, such as dust, pollen, and mould spores, from the air. In an HVAC system, coils are used to transfer heat between the air and the refrigerant. Utilising blowers to circulate air throughout the system. Controls are used to regulate the air handler's temperature and operation.

Registers are HVAC system components that distribute conditioned air throughout a building. Registers can be mounted on the floor or the wall and are available in a variety of materials, such as metal, plastic, and wood. The size and location of the registers are determined by the building's scale, architecture, and HVAC system design.

Registers are comprised of a shutter, a damper, and a diffuser. The visible portion of the register that conceals the ventilation aperture is the grille. The damper is utilised to control the airflow through the register. The diffuser is utilised to distribute air throughout the space.

Zoning

Zoning is an optional but advantageous element of distribution system design. Different zones of a building can be independently conditioned, which can increase energy efficiency and occupant comfort. Through the use of multiple thermostats and dampers in the ventilation system, it is possible to create zones.

Installation and Maintenance of System

Installation and maintenance are crucial to the efficacy and endurance of a distribution system. Installation must be performed by a licenced and experienced HVAC technician in accordance with local building codes and manufacturer guidelines. Regular maintenance, such as air filter replacement and system cleansing, can help ensure the optimal performance and longevity of a distribution system.

Installation, maintenance, and repair of heating systems

Heating systems must have proper installation, maintenance, and repair for optimal performance and longevity. In this chapter, we will examine the fundamentals of heating system installation, maintenance, and repair, including the significance of employing a licenced and seasoned HVAC technician and adhering to local building codes and manufacturer specifications.

Installation

For heating systems to operate safely and efficiently, proper installation is required. Installation must be performed by a licenced and experienced HVAC technician in accordance with local building codes and manufacturer guidelines.

The HVAC technician will supervise the placement and installation of heating equipment, such as a furnace, boiler, or heat pump, during the installation process. The technician will also ensure that the equipment is appropriately scaled and that the ductwork and distribution system are designed to satisfy the building's heating capacity specifications.

Maintenance

Heating systems require routine maintenance for optimal performance and longevity. Maintenance should be performed by a licenced and seasoned HVAC technician, and should consist of the following:

Dirty air filters can restrict circulation and reduce the effectiveness of a heating system. Air filters should be regularly inspected and replaced in accordance with the manufacturer's instructions.

Dust, grime, and detritus can accumulate in the heating equipment and distribution system, reducing the heating system's efficiency and increasing the likelihood of equipment failure. Regular system maintenance can help guarantee the optimal performance and longevity of a heating system.

Components such as belts, pulleys, and motors should be routinely inspected, and any deteriorated or damaged components should be replaced without delay. The HVAC technician must calibrate and modify the controls and sensors of the heating system to ensure accurate and efficient operation. The HVAC technician should conduct a combustion analysis on fuel-burning heating systems to ensure that they are operating safely and efficiently.

Repair

Heating systems will inevitably require maintenance at some stage during their lifetime. The following tasks should be performed by a licenced and experienced HVAC technician:

- Problem identification: The HVAC technician will identify the problem with the heating system by testing components, inspecting the equipment, and analysing system data.

- Component replacement: The HVAC technician will replace any deteriorated or broken components, including sensors, actuators, and pulleys.
- The HVAC technician will calibrate and modify the controls and sensors of the heating system to ensure accurate and efficient operation.
- The HVAC technician will evaluate the heating system to ensure that it is operating effectively and safely.

Troubleshooting common heating issues

There are numerous issues that can affect the efficacy and efficiency of heating systems. In this chapter, we will examine the most common heating problems and their troubleshooting solutions, including thermostat, ventilation, and heating equipment problems.

Problems with the Thermostat Thermostat problems are a common cause of heating system problems. The heating system may turn on and off erratically or fail to turn on altogether if the thermostat is malfunctioning. Typical thermostat problems include:

- A thermostat that is filthy or malfunctioning can cause the system to malfunction. The thermostat should be regularly cleansed and, if necessary, replaced.
- Incorrect thermostat settings Incorrect thermostat settings, such as a low temperature setting, can prevent the system from starting or cause it to shut down prematurely.
- Loose or faulty wiring: Loose or faulty cabling can cause the thermostat to malfunction and the system to fail to turn on or shut down prematurely.

Airflow Problems

Heating system issues can also be caused by airflow issues. Inadequate ventilation can cause the heating system to work harder than required, thereby decreasing its efficacy and increasing energy costs. Common circulation problems include:

- Air filters that are dirty can restrict circulation and reduce the heating system's efficiency. Air filters should be regularly inspected and replaced in accordance with the manufacturer's instructions.

- Blocked or closed registers: Blocked or closed registers can reduce the heating system's efficacy by restricting ventilation. Registers must be routinely inspected and kept spotless and unobstructed.

- Leaky ducts: Leaky ducts can enable heated air to escape, reducing the heating system's efficiency. Ducts should be routinely inspected and rectified as needed.

Heating Equipment Issues

Problems with the heating system can also be caused by problems with the heating apparatus. Common problems with heating equipment include:

- Burners that are dirty or malfunctioning can cause the heating system to operate inefficiently or not at all. Burners should be routinely inspected and, if necessary, cleansed or replaced.

- A malfunctioning ignition system can prevent the heating system from functioning at all. The ignition system should be routinely inspected and, if necessary, repaired or replaced.

- Low refrigerant levels: Low refrigerant levels can reduce the efficiency of a heat pump. Refrigerant levels should be inspected frequently and replenished as needed.

Book 5: Advanced HVAC Technology

Energy efficiency and cost savings in HVAC technology

In HVAC technology, energy efficiency and cost savings are crucial considerations. A significant portion of energy consumption in commercial and residential buildings is accounted for by HVAC systems; increasing the energy efficacy of these systems can reduce energy costs and environmental impact. In this chapter, we will examine the principles of energy efficiency and cost savings in HVAC technology, including the implementation of energy-saving strategies and the use of high-efficiency equipment.

High-Efficiency Machinery

Comparing high-efficiency HVAC equipment to standard equipment can result in considerable energy savings. Examples of efficient equipment include:

Furnaces with high efficiency: Furnaces with high efficiency use advanced combustion technology to produce more heat with less fuel. This can result in substantial energy savings in comparison to conventional furnaces.

High-efficiency boilers: High-efficiency boilers use advanced technology to extract more heat from the fuel than conventional boilers, resulting in significant energy savings.

High-efficiency heat pumps: High-efficiency heat pumps employ innovative technology to provide heating and ventilation while consuming less energy. This can result in substantial energy savings in comparison to conventional heat pumps.

Variable-speed equipment, such as variable-speed compressors and pumps, can modify their output to match the building's heating or cooling demand, resulting in energy savings.

Energy-Saving Strategies

In addition to high-efficiency equipment, numerous energy-saving strategies can be implemented to increase the energy efficiency of HVAC systems. Examples of typical energy-saving strategies include:

Programmable thermostats can be set to modify the building's temperature based on occupancy and usage patterns. This can lead to substantial energy savings in comparison to manual thermostats.

Zoning: Zoning permits various areas of a building to be independently heated or chilled based on occupancy and usage patterns. This can result in substantial energy savings compared to simultaneously heating or chilling the complete building.

Air sealing and insulation can reduce heat loss and gain through the building envelope, thereby reducing the heating and cooling burden on the HVAC system and resulting in energy savings.

Regular maintenance: Regular maintenance, such as replacing air filters and cleansing the system, can help ensure optimal HVAC system performance and efficiency, leading to energy savings.

Renewable energy: HVAC systems can be powered by renewable energy sources such as solar panels and geothermal systems, resulting in significant energy savings and environmental benefits.

Principles of HVAC system design for DIYers

DIYers can design and implement HVAC systems if they have the necessary knowledge and equipment. HVAC system design can be a complex and technical procedure. This chapter will examine the principles of HVAC system design for do-it-yourselfers, including the fundamentals of HVAC system design, the required tools and materials, and the processes for designing and installing an HVAC system.

Introduction to HVAC System Design

The function of an HVAC system is to provide a building with heating, ventilation, and air conditioning. The heating system, the cooling system, and the ventilation system are the three primary components of an HVAC system. The heating system may consist of a furnace or boiler, and the cooling system may consist of an air conditioner or heat pump. The ventilation system provides the building with fresh air and may consist of ducting, air filtration, and blowers.

Required Materials and Equipment

The design and installation of an HVAC system requires the use of specialised equipment and components. Among the instruments and materials that do-it-yourselfers may require are:

- Software for HVAC Design HVAC design software can assist do-it-yourselfers in calculating heating and cooling loads, sizing equipment, and designing ductwork configurations.
- A tape measure is required for determining the dimensions of the building and the location of the apparatus.
- Distribution of heated or chilled air throughout a building requires ductwork.
- The facility requires HVAC apparatus, such as a furnace, air conditioner, or heat pump, to provide heating and ventilation.
- Electrical Wiring: Electrical wiring is required to connect HVAC equipment to the electrical system of the building.

Steps in HVAC System Design

There are several stages involved in designing and installing an HVAC system. DIY HVAC system design is comprised of the following steps:

Calculate the heating and cooling loads in Step 1.

The first step in designing an HVAC system is calculating the building's heating and ventilation demands. This involves determining the building's heat gain and heat loss, which are affected by factors such as the building's scale and orientation, the number of occupants, and the insulation levels.

Step 2: Select Equipment

After calculating the heating and cooling demands, the next stage is to select the proper HVAC apparatus for the building. The apparatus should be sized to match the heating and cooling loads of the building and selected based on efficacy, cost, and compatibility with the electrical system of the building.

Step 3: Design the Ductwork Layout

The architecture of the ductwork is a crucial aspect of HVAC system design, as it determines how heated or chilled air is distributed throughout the building. Taking into consideration building layout, apparatus location, and airflow requirements, the ductwork configuration should be designed to provide optimal airflow and temperature distribution.

Step 4: Install the Equipment and Ductwork

After designing the equipment and ductwork configuration, the subsequent phase is to implement the equipment and ductwork. This entails connecting the equipment to the building's electrical system, installing the ductwork, and verifying the system's functionality.

Step 5: System Maintenance

Regular maintenance is an integral component of the design of HVAC systems, as it ensures optimal system performance and longevity. Regular maintenance tasks for do-it-yourselfers include replacing air filters, cleaning equipment, and inspecting ductwork for leakage and damage.

Building a custom HVAC system to meet your unique needs

Every building has unique heating and cooling requirements, which can be met by a custom HVAC system. A customised HVAC system can offer greater comfort, energy efficiency, and cost savings than a standard HVAC system. In this chapter, we will discuss the stages involved in designing and installing a custom HVAC system, including identifying heating and cooling requirements, selecting equipment, and designing and implementing the system.

Determining Heating and Cooling Requirements

The first step in designing a custom HVAC system is determining the building's heating and ventilation requirements. This includes the scale and configuration of the building, the number of occupants, the desired temperature range, and the energy efficiency objectives of the building. This information can be obtained through an energy audit of the building or a consultation with an HVAC expert.

Choosing Equipment

After determining the heating and cooling requirements of the building, the next stage is to select the appropriate equipment for the custom HVAC system. The equipment selection should take into account the heating and cooling loads of the building, the intended level of efficiency, and the project budget. High-efficiency furnaces, boilers, heat pumps, air conditioners, and ventilation systems are among the equipment options.

Conception of the System

After the apparatus has been chosen, the custom HVAC system must be designed. This includes devising the ductwork layout, selecting the appropriate controls and thermostats, and sizing the equipment. The design should take into account the layout and orientation of the building, the location of the apparatus, and the intended ventilation and temperature distribution.

Installation

After designing a custom HVAC system, the final stage is to install the system. This includes testing and calibrating the system and installing the equipment, ductwork, controls, and thermostats. To ensure that the installation is performed correctly and safely, it is essential to employ a licenced and seasoned HVAC professional.

Advantages of a Tailored HVAC System

A custom HVAC system can offer a variety of advantages over a prefabricated HVAC system. Several of these advantages include:

- A custom HVAC system can be designed to provide optimal comfort and temperature control for the building's particular requirements.
- Enhanced Energy Efficiency: A custom HVAC system can be designed to be extremely energy efficient, resulting in lower energy costs and a smaller environmental footprint.
- A custom HVAC system can provide long-term cost savings through lower energy expenses, reduced maintenance costs, and a longer equipment duration.
- A custom HVAC system can include sophisticated air filtration and ventilation systems, resulting in a healthier indoor environment and enhanced indoor air quality.

Emerging trends in HVAC technology and their potential impact on the industry

Every year sees the introduction of new technologies and innovations in the HVAC industry. These emerging trends have the potential to have a significant impact on the industry, from enhancing energy efficiency and indoor air quality to altering the design and installation of HVAC systems. In this chapter, we will examine some emerging HVAC technology trends and their potential impact on the industry.

Smart HVAC Systems

Intelligent HVAC systems are one of the most significant emerging HVAC technology trends. Utilising sensors, data analytics, and automation, these systems optimise HVAC performance and decrease energy consumption. Smart HVAC systems may include features such as learning thermostats, which can adjust temperature settings automatically based on user behaviour, and occupancy sensors, which can detect when a room is occupied and alter heating and cooling accordingly. These systems may also be incorporated with building automation systems for enhanced control and efficiency.

Integration of Renewable Energy Technologies

Integration of renewable energy is another emergent trend in HVAC technology. As solar and wind energy become more affordable and accessible, HVAC systems are being designed to take advantage of these technologies. Renewable energy can be used to directly power HVAC systems or to mitigate energy consumption via net metering or energy storage. This trend has the potential to substantially reduce energy costs and environmental impact, while providing building proprietors with greater energy independence.

Innovative Air Filtration

Building owners and occupants are increasingly concerned about indoor air quality, and advanced air filtration is an emergent trend in HVAC technology that addresses this concern. Advanced air filtration systems utilise high-efficiency filters and air purifiers to eliminate airborne contaminants such as bacteria, viruses, and allergens. These systems may also include UV-C lamps and ionisers, which can enhance air quality even further. Advanced air filtration has the potential to enhance the health and comfort of building occupants while preventing the spread of airborne diseases.

Ductless HVAC Techniques

Emerging in HVAC technology, ductless HVAC systems provide greater flexibility and efficacy than conventional HVAC systems. Instead of relying on ductwork to distribute air throughout a building, ductless systems rely on individual air handlers to provide heating and conditioning to specific rooms or zones. This can result in increased energy efficiency, as less energy is lost due to ductwork leakage and inefficiencies. In addition to being simpler to install and maintain than conventional HVAC systems, ductless systems are a popular choice for retrofit projects and new construction.

Reality, Virtual and Augmented

Virtual and augmented reality are emerging technologies that have the potential to transform the design, installation, and maintenance of HVAC systems. These technologies can be used to construct virtual models of HVAC systems, allowing designers and installers to visualise and evaluate the efficacy of the system prior to its installation. Virtual and augmented reality can also be used to train and support HVAC technicians, allowing them to more precisely diagnose and remedy problems.

HVAC automation, control, and monitoring systems

Automation, control, and monitoring systems are crucial components of contemporary HVAC systems, allowing for greater efficiency, comfort, and control. These systems use sensors, controls, and software to monitor and adjust HVAC performance based on a number of variables, including temperature, humidity, occupancy, and energy demand. In this chapter, we will examine the benefits, components, and applications of HVAC automation, control, and monitoring systems.

HVAC Automation, Control, and Monitoring System Benefits

HVAC automation, control, and monitoring systems provide numerous advantages for building proprietors, occupants, and HVAC specialists. Several of these advantages include:

- Energy Efficiency: Automation, control, and monitoring systems for HVAC can optimise HVAC performance in order to reduce energy consumption and costs.

- Automation and control systems can give building occupants greater control over temperature, humidity, and air quality, resulting in greater comfort.
- Monitoring systems can detect and diagnose HVAC problems with greater speed and accuracy, allowing for more efficient maintenance and repairs.

By ensuring optimal performance and reducing wear and tear, automation and monitoring systems can assist in extending the life of HVAC equipment.

Components of HVAC Control, Monitoring, and Automation Systems

The components of HVAC automation, control, and monitoring systems include sensors, controls, software, and communication networks. Among the essential components of these systems are:

- Temperature, humidity, air quality, and occupancy are some of the HVAC performance parameters that sensors monitor. Thermostats, humidity sensors, CO_2 sensors, and occupancy sensors are examples of these sensors.
- Controls: Controls are utilised to adjust HVAC performance based on sensor data. Thermostats, variable frequency motors, and building automation systems are examples of these controls.
- Software: Software is used to analyse and interpret data collected by sensors and controllers, enabling greater HVAC

performance optimisation and control. This software may include energy management systems and software for building automation.

- Communication Networks: Communication networks are utilised to link sensors, controls, and software to enable real-time monitoring and control of HVAC performance. These networks may include both wired and wireless connections and are compatible with building automation systems.

HVAC Automation, Control, and Monitoring System Applications

There are numerous applications for HVAC automation, control, and monitoring systems, ranging from residential residences to large commercial structures. These are some of the most prevalent applications for these systems:

- With features such as programmable thermostats and zoning systems, automation and control systems can be used in residential residences to provide greater comfort and energy efficiency.
- Automation, control, and monitoring systems are frequently used in commercial buildings to optimise HVAC performance and reduce energy costs, with features including building automation systems and variable frequency actuators.
- Automation, control, and monitoring systems can also be utilised in industrial facilities, such as factories and warehouses, to

provide optimal HVAC performance and energy efficiency through the use of process control systems and energy management systems.

HVAC maintenance and service contracts

Automation, control, and monitoring systems are crucial components of contemporary HVAC systems, allowing for greater efficiency, comfort, and control. These systems use sensors, controls, and software to monitor and adjust HVAC performance based on a number of variables, including temperature, humidity, occupancy, and energy demand. In this chapter, we will examine the benefits, components, and applications of HVAC automation, control, and monitoring systems.

HVAC Automation, Control, and Monitoring System Benefits

HVAC automation, control, and monitoring systems provide numerous advantages for building proprietors, occupants, and HVAC specialists. Several of these advantages include:

- Energy Efficiency: Automation, control, and monitoring systems for HVAC can optimise HVAC performance in order to reduce energy consumption and costs.

- Automation and control systems can give building occupants greater control over temperature, humidity, and air quality, resulting in greater comfort.

- Monitoring systems can detect and diagnose HVAC problems with greater speed and accuracy, allowing for more efficient maintenance and repairs.

- By ensuring optimal performance and reducing wear and tear, automation and monitoring systems can assist in extending the life of HVAC equipment.

Components of HVAC Control, Monitoring, and Automation Systems

The components of HVAC automation, control, and monitoring systems include sensors, controls, software, and communication networks. Among the essential components of these systems are:

- Temperature, humidity, air quality, and occupancy are some of the HVAC performance parameters that sensors monitor. Thermostats, humidity sensors, CO_2 sensors, and occupancy sensors are examples of these sensors.

- Controls: Controls are utilised to adjust HVAC performance based on sensor data. Thermostats, variable frequency motors, and building automation systems are examples of these controls.

- Software: Software is used to analyse and interpret data collected by sensors and controllers, enabling greater HVAC performance optimisation and control. This software may include energy management systems and software for building automation.

- Communication Networks: Communication networks are utilised to link sensors, controls, and software to enable real-time monitoring and control of HVAC performance. These networks may include both wired and wireless connections and are compatible with building automation systems.

HVAC Automation, Control, and Monitoring System Applications

There are numerous applications for HVAC automation, control, and monitoring systems, ranging from residential residences to large commercial structures. These are some of the most prevalent applications for these systems:

With features such as programmable thermostats and zoning systems, automation and control systems can be used in residential residences to provide greater comfort and energy efficiency.

Automation, control, and monitoring systems are frequently used in commercial buildings to optimise HVAC performance and reduce energy costs, with features including building automation systems and variable frequency actuators.

Automation, control, and monitoring systems can also be utilised in industrial facilities, such as factories and warehouses, to provide optimal HVAC performance and energy efficiency through the use of process control systems and energy management systems.

Made in the USA
Las Vegas, NV
05 September 2023

76997289R00061